Increase Your Confidence
in One Day...

Increase Your Confidence in One Day...

and Stay Confident for the Rest of Your Life!

Olga Levancuka

Cover photograph © Katie Hyams 2010

Increase Your Confidence in One Day and Stay Confident for the Rest of Your Life, Olga Levancuka.

For bulk purchases for sales promotions, premiums, fund-raising, or educational use please inquire via www.SkinnyRichCoach.com

ISBN 978-1-4461-6602-4

Confidence is that feeling by which the mind embarks in great and honorable courses with a sure hope and trust in itself.

Marcus T. Cicero

"What can I tell you about Olga?
Possible one of the best individual's I have had the privilege to meet. I was introduced to Olga some years ago and as much as I liked her, I cannot honestly say I knew her.
This changed about a year ago when I was invited to join Olga's workshops, focussing on different aspects on how to enhance one's life and achieve what you want, looking at Happiness, Love, Confidence, Money, Abundance, Language, I could go on and on...
Some of the issues addressed were very personal. However, Olga created a safe environment, where issues could be broken down and examined, helping us finding our own solutions.
My respect, trust and admiration of Olga is huge. Not only how Olga conducted the classes, with a firm, gentle manner but also the knowledge she imparted has not only changed my perceptions in my career and life, but what is possible and for that I am immeasurably grateful."

Marie Elaine
Civil Servant
Department of Health

"I have known Olga for almost a decade now. She is an amazing woman with endless positive energy. During this time, she has been a genuine friend. Any advice she has provided has always been very straight talking, there is no 'beating around the bush' yet provided in a positive, caring and impartial manner.

When I first went to Olga's workshop, I attended out of loyalty as a friend and a sceptic. However, over the course of the workshops, I couldn't help becoming infected by Olga's positivity and the lessons given. I now have to concede that her courses really made a difference. Olga and her courses really energised me to 'get off my backside' and change from a person who is full off 'thoughts about actions ' to a person who 'actions my thoughts'. Thank you Olga."

K Skinner
Equuleus Solutions Ltd

"Olga is amazing and I'm so happy to have her in my life!
We met when I was going through my divorce and even though I'm confident in business, being the CEO/Creative Director for WOWBOW London, this change in my personal life really knock me sideways.
Olga has this uncanny ability to make you see things so clearly as well as point out positive actions one can take to get you back to standing tall and be the woman you are destined to be.
It is not only in what she tells you but also what she shows you in just the way she is. Olga is beautiful inside and out.
Not only does she talk the talk, but she also walks the walk......and that walk is tall, confident, feminine and strong.

She is a true inspiration and I always look forward to my time with her .....or as love to call it as my Dose O' Olga!!!

Kim Bull
Founder/Creative Director
WOWBOW
www.wowbow.co.uk

"I have been very fortunate in my life to get to know and be inspired by the lovely author of this book.
If you have picked this book up be sure to add it to your collection.
Olga has a great gift & by reading this book you will be able to share her gift to enhance your life.
Without lecturing Olga will guide you to a new level of confidence.
If you read the feed back from Olga's workshops you will quickly realise I am not on my own with my admiration for her very special unique work."

Louise Bysouth
M.D.
www.swiggiesuk.com
The 21st Century Drink Bottle For All

"Taking on too much projects and getting confused in the process is a big issue for me as an entrepreneur.
Olga helped and guide me by always asking important questions to make me think of what steps to take next. She has also helped me in being more efficient (in my time and budgets) for managing my business.
London is a really competitive place for fashion people and she had given me the confidence to stay in the game."

Noni Zulkifli
Founder
www.imagic-styling.com

"Meeting Olga in person is a real pleasure. She is a dynamic individual that not only inspires you, breathes new life into you, but truly motivates you to reach your dreams and helps you understand why....
You know when you meet someone special, and Olga is one extremely special person.
She helps you understand how to achieve what may have been alluding you...She is magic!
...When I am inspired by Olga, the energy is magic! I can do anything!
Olga offers not only great advice, but puts you in the best mood for achieving all of your dreams making it effortless."

Dr. Jamie Hampton DAOM
Founder
www.berkeleygoldenleaf.com

"Olga has a real zest for life and her enthusiasm in helping others to break free and 'get it' as she does, is second to none!
Her 'Confidence' seminars are top-class. Full of great motivational content with realistic goals, and so sensitively put together by someone who clearly has a commitment to making others feel better about their lives...It is a pleasure to have known Olga."

Julia Kent
Owner
The Best of Westminster

Contents

One of the Most Individual Books on Confidence Ever Written

This Unique Book is most beneficial when treated as a Workbook. *Confidence* is a feeling we create and keep while being in constant progress. For that reason the book contains exercises which can boost your confidence almost at once. Some exercises stated here are performed during the Confidence Workshops run by the author yet adjusted for the reader.

The book can become your constant companion as the exercises described here are timeless and will apply to any situation in your life when a boost of confidence is vital. You may choose the ones that work best for you after reading the whole book, yet it is best to perform each of the exercises described in the book at least a few times as you may find some exercises are more suited to a particular state you are in at a given time.

The way the language is used here, your confidence level may increase just by reading it.

The author is well known for working with successful entrepreneurs, who are constantly featured on TV and in press worldwide, yet additionally working with a small number of people helping them to come out of depression and supporting them to move forward, partly due to the author's personal life experience.

The wealth of experience the author has, means that the exercises and text in the book are equally applicable to successful entrepreneurs who would like to take a next important step in their career and to a student looking to start a new career, who may have an important job interview the next day, as well as to a housewife whose capability to manage everyday chores may impress any CEO, yet who feels intimidated when the matter applies to her personal interests.

If at any stage of your life you believe you need a confidence boost — the book is for You!

The author is very privileged to help many and it is a truly unique opportunity to share such great knowledge and experience with you, the readers.

Preface

Olga helped me when I was writing my most recent book, and so when she asked me to write the preface for her book, I jumped at the opportunity.

Why is confidence important? It is such an intangible property yet absolutely central to a successful life. Talent is not enough — it is the ability to act, to DO that really sorts out the people that get things done from ineffectual dreamers who have wonderful ideas but never manage to complete anything.

Of course it is easy to find reasons not to do things; and the problem is especially acute when what you are trying to do is exceptional, when your goal is something extraordinary. When you go against the received wisdom, you will be surrounded by people telling you that what you are trying to do is impossible, or impractical, or too hard. What makes you special? What makes you think that you can achieve what other people have only dreamed of?

But of course, these are not reasons at all. Everything has to be done for the first time once; any worthwhile achievement is going to be difficult and hard, and the difficulty of the task can sometimes appear to be a compelling reason not to do it.

It's important to combine a rational assessment of what it is you are trying to do with the emotional resources that you need to overcome the perception of the difficulty of the task. It is that source of emotional energy to solve problems, to be positive even when facing obstacles that may appear to be impossibly difficult, that is "confidence".

Even the most confident among us need a boost sometimes;

a sequence of setbacks can knock the stuffing out of us, and start us thinking about all of the ways that we can fail.

Olga has had several successful careers already and her experience in running businesses and building rapidly growing enterprises is a testimony to her energy and her ability to act, and follow through on her actions.

She has a very clear idea of people's motivations and a very accurate,

almost uncanny intuition about the right levers to pull to help people to see inside themselves.

Some if not most self-help books consist largely of "New Age" platitudes about the power of positive thinking. Olga doesn't take that path in her work; rather she recognises the power of the mind, and the feedback between one's mental state and the interactions, sometimes subconscious with other people; the way on which ones psychological state is communicated to others through rather subtle means, posture or body-language, the words we use, and so on.

Without lapsing into mysticism, she still manages to communicate these ideas in an engaging and non-technical way.

I have seen the success of her coaching techniques on people first hand;

Olga has an amazing talent for change. Whether the change you are looking for is a transformation in the way you manage a company, or a more personal relationship-oriented goal, Olga can deliver.

This book is quite inspiring — it's an overused cliche to say that it will change your life, but it just might.

Alex Clark
Royal Holloway, University of London

Acknowledgments

This book owes an enormous debt, as do I,
   to my father for constant belief in me,
   to my departed husband Lambros for teaching me what life is about,
   to Alexander who is simply accepting and loving me exactly the way I am.

From the Author

I have rebuilt my life by using many exercises I shall describe in this book. I need to warn you some of the exercises are so powerful that by applying them during my sessions I have succeeded in helping many clients while they were coming off anti-depressants.

Some skills were perfected when learning new methods of self-help and applying them to my clients who run several businesses in order to keep work/life balance stable and yes, I will be sharing them with you in this book as well.

Via this book I will show you how to regain your *confidence* at any stage of your life. No matter what you have been through, no matter how low or how unconfident you feel yourself at certain situations, I shall give you the skills and knowledge to constantly stay confident.

I also ask you to promote this book. Let more people have access to such unique information. We want our friends and people we know to enjoy their life as well.

Introduction

Many of you when meeting me are amazed at how confident I am and how successful my business is, what an amazing lifestyle and truly unique friends I have.

Many of my clients and friends have been asking me to share the secrets I know regarding confidence or to be more precise how to increase confidence when they need it most.

After running Happiness Workshops for over a year and multiple workshops on "How to Increase Your income for Entrepreneurs", it became clear that confidence plays a vital role in my clients' success rate.

At first I have included just some materials on confidence into my existing sessions, yet later it became clear that a separate workshop for increasing confidence is an absolutely must for any person before taking further action.

You can have many needs and many desires, yet it is almost impossible to achieve success without *confidence*.

That's the story how the Skinny Rich Coach became known as the Confidence Guru and is always on my clients minds when the word *confidence* appears in conversation.

Regarding myself personally, I was once asked by a client:

'What's your story?'.

I have to admit, I was taken by surprise as I have never even considered my previous life experience as important: I am a type of person who truly enjoys the present, nor did I think my past life could be of any interest to my clients. How wrong was I? More and more clients ask me this question recently.

Of course I have a story ... in one way or another, we all have something we would like to call a story, it may be our award winning event we want to constantly shout about to the world, or on the other hand a special occasion which turned out wrong, either our difficult relationship with our parents or for some a loss of a family member. It is life, and life is a constantly moving chain of events.

Have you ever met a 100% life-proof person? I did not; if you did - forward me their details so that I congratulate them in person and observe them to learn their secrets... or may be not. There is something priceless in experiencing life exactly as it is, staying in control of some events while letting others appear unexpectedly.

...for most of us, we have to overcome certain life situations, whether we like or not the pain we receive, there are some things we simply can't avoid. And bear in mind, the pain I refer to may be physical or emotional or both.

I thought for a while at that meeting when the question was asked for the first time and I have shared my story at last, outside of my friends and family circle. I shall share it with you shortly too.

Increase Your Confidence in One Day... and Stay Confident for the Rest of Your Life!

We are conditioned to complain from childhood.

Just pay attention closely every time you see a child and parents. How much more attention does a child usually get when is hurt? All of it (usually)! ... And how much attention does the child get when he or she happily plays games? — hardly any, I doubt the child wants any attention when so busy having fun.

Yet the conditioning is happening. The child gets upset, there is attention. You get upset at school, you normally get attention. And so on. We learn, we get conditioned to the fact that if we want attention — we need to complain.

That transfers into adulthood; the more fun we have the less we complain, we stop having fun, we want attention? Naturally we complain. In fact we complain so much that we start to forget why we even do it. It becomes a habit.

Have you ever been in a situation at a party when you felt uncomfortable? There are hardly any people you know yet the host is way too busy to introduce you?

You move away a bit, hoping the host will notice and come to your rescue. No, it does not happen; then you find a secluded place hoping (more like screaming out loud in your mind!) someone will notice you. Someone will start talking to you. Someone will find out how cool you are and introduce you to everyone else. No-one paid attention and you left the party unnoticed.

Once at home you are confused as to why you even bothered to go to the party. Why were you hoping to meet new cool people when no one ever notices you. You continue beating up yourself emotionally. You start blaming yourself. You think you are not interesting enough, people do not respect you. No one cares about you... Later you start believing all those negative thoughts that you planted yourself! and start acting like an unsuccessful, unloved person (the phone is still ringing, and some people are still inviting you... yet you choose to believe your own thoughts therefore you assume they are just calling out of politeness).

And so on...

What happens in reality, is that no one is aware you are feeling that way. Everyone is having fun! They do not want to spoil their fun by giving attention to someone looking grumpy in a corner. In fact some friends might even try for a short while only to regret later.

What you want to realise and more importantly remember, is that we give away a lot on a subconscious level. You might not realise it, yet your thoughts are louder than actions. Your own body will send out a zillion signals to everyone projecting the very thoughts you think, as an unthoughtful traitor.

Yes, we might not exactly know your thoughts... still (as you have guessed by now) we pick up your signals on a subconscious level.

As much as we want to come over and talk to you, our receptors send 'warning' signals that keep us right where we are enjoying ourselves or at least avoiding your area.

But enough about out unhappy partying experiences, let me divert your attention. We are here to *increase your confidence* after all. You know why you need *confidence*, you don't need me to tell you why it's great to stay confident. What about *self-confidence*?

I once heard this amazing story I have shared with many of my clients as well as my colleagues; and now I am sharing it here with you.

Many people still refer to this story when feeling low on self-confidence or just want to remind themselves about qualities they forget they have.

I've been told about an elderly lady leaving somewhere in Wales in a lovely cottage. Unfortunately her lovely cottage was so far away from any town she had no opportunity to have a mains water supply. And so every day, she went to a small lake with her two pots, filled them with water and brought them back home.

The lake wasn't too far away but the path was rather interesting, it was slightly dry and dusty on one side.

One of the pots was old and had a crack and the other one was slightly newer and had no problems at all, or as we say: it was perfect. The crack in the older pot wasn't small, in fact it leaked so badly that by the time the pots with water were brought back to the cottage, the older pot had only half the water left that the old lady had filled it with.

The older pot was so upset and felt such guilt for making the old lady carry it all the way back to the cottage only to arrive half full. The pot lost all the confidence it had and thought of itself not only as a worthless pot but as one inflicting pain on the old lady.

One day the older pot shared its fears with the newer pot asking for some sort of support and seeking any solutions to help the old lady and save itself from its embarrassing existence. As you can believe, the shiny newer pot only laughed and made the older pot feel even worse about the whole situation.

After a few months had passed and it was coming close to the end of the summer the older pot decided to find whatever bravery it could in itself and to approach the old lady itself. Once the old lady had filled the pots with water that day and started her walk back to the little cottage, the broken pot spoke:

> "My dear old lady I am so sorry to put you through so much trouble and not being able to serve you well. I am very humiliated I am not serving you as well as I should. I realize I am at the worst stage of my existence and I believe it would be only fair to you to end my shame and guilt."

The old lady was so surprised, she almost shouted:

> "Dear pot, did you not notice I always carry you on this side of the road so that on the way back to the cottage you always water the grass and little flowers? Did you not pay attention to how dry and dusty the other side of the path is?
> Did you not realize those field flowers I bring home every week and they keep me so happy for days are those very flowers you water? If it wasn't for your crack you are so ashamed of, I would not enjoy these flowers, I would not enjoy the sweet and amazing smell of them.
> If it wasn't for you being exactly as you are, I would have a boring walk on a dusty path back home every time after the lake and I would not cherish the moments of noticing how new flowers start blossoming at different times?
> My dear old pot, not only you are so important and much needed. You are absolutely perfect exactly the way you are!"

The old lady and those two pots are still together, although now both pots know how each of them is very special in their unique ways.

Pause for few minutes. Think of yourself, think of our own unique qualities that you have which you might have forgotten about. Write them down. Which ones made you happiest?

NOTES:

_____

_____

_____

_____

_____

_____

_____

_____

_____

_____

_____

_____

You are not the only one. Everybody forgets how great they are sometimes. We always pay attention to how great or weak is our opponent, yet we are not used to think of ourselves in a better 'light'.

Of course we all have weaknesses yet we all have something great and unique! Change your attention. By shifting your attention to your great qualities, people will start forgetting about your weaknesses. If you do that continuously, re-read this book after a year and you will notice that you have forgotten all about your weaknesses, almost as if you had never had them before.

I am glad you are back with yourself now or at least on the starting line to finding your true new self. What's next?

You may say, ok, I feel a bit better, yet still no changes are happening in my life?

Every time we change our thoughts or attention we need to support them with actions, no matter how big or small. Before we get to action stage let's jump ahead and mention procrastination...

It is easy for some to start believing they can do or achieve anything only to get comfortable and get stuck in the procrastination stage.

How do you deal with that?

That's where coaching is a must.

As a personal development coach has just the techniques to reconfirm with your subconscious whether the goals you have set are truly yours. If they are not, it would be very difficult for you to stay motivated unless you are running away from something. Even so, the great coach can motivate you there too.

However sometimes it is difficult to get off your 'back' and really start doing it.

As a coach I always elicit those much needed motives.

After such an inception, your actions and results will evolve dramatically.

For those of you reading the book and considering taking matters into your own hands - I would like to congratulate you! That is exactly what you did by becoming an owner of this book.

You are coaching yourself right now.

Now, think of at least one reason you really need to improve your *confidence* for?

What will increased *confidence* help you achieve?

When is the next event you could apply your newly acquired *confidence* to?

NOTES:

_____

_____

_____

_____

_____

_____

_____

_____

_____

_____

_____

_____

Let's continue...

The way the book is structured is very similar to the confidence workshops I run. Why? Because there are plenty of books which spend most of their pages just explaining you why it is important to increase your confidence.

I know, you know best why you need to increase your confidence — You do not need me to explain that to you and that is the reason you are holding this book ♥

That is one of the reasons this book is great for people who just want to take their life to next level, to achieve new results or improve their existing relationship, start their own business or run their 5000 employee company with less effort and more confidence, or simply to achieve the ideal work/life balance or even just to find a job.

I offer you a very straightforward and unique way of looking at the every day issues we would like to face with more confidence. It is almost like providing you with daily mind exercises; introducing you to a mini-gym for your mind.

I will give you skills to let you stay in control of your feelings of confidence.

So expect amazing fun and great results by following the exercises.

I've been through a lot yet I managed to come back on top and have a fantastic life filled with joy, fun and laughter.

I wish you the same and I am here to support you on achieving your desires and help you to avoid any troubles you would normally have to face due to lack of *confidence*.

During my confidence workshops people interact with each other constantly and I am always astonished how easily they do it and absolutely enjoy it. Let's face it - they came because they wanted to *increase their confidence*.

Do you know how sometimes it is so easy to speak to a person without even realising it?

When asked my workshops attendees said: 'It might be easy because we don't know each other.'

And that is true for many cases when you are meeting people under circumstances when mutual interests are at play. You neutralise a few major barriers including the social ones.

You know how sometimes you meet a new person and without any conversation you already like the person. The opposite can be true.

Let's be honest we all love compliments and positive feedback. We all want and crave recognition. Yes, we are human beings yet we are social animals. A need to be recognised lies at the base of our survival.

We do not want to be excluded from the group, we want to belong and we want to feel needed, so that the group does keep us as a member. It is necessary for our continued human existence.

Sometimes we try to fit in too hard, we ignore the fact other members are doing the same. We pay more attention to criticism as we constantly are afraid of being 'excluded'. There is even a valid explanation to why this shyness was needed in a primitive age, simply for the reason that 'weaker' members did not want to draw any attention to themselves to ensure that they stayed within the group, being protected from other humans or wild animals.

Those times are over! Yet the habits have stayed.

Such inherited needs and habits cost us dear.

We are so used to paying attention to criticism nowadays, we overlook the compliments we receive and we stop recognising the great qualities we have.

Exercise 1.

Think of the last compliment you remember at the moment.

Write it down.

Now, which was the last positive feedback you have received? Note it down as well.

During today pay attention to any compliment or positive remark you receive and note it down every time it makes you feel great about yourself or even puts a smile on your face or your heart ☺

Use NOTES here to write them down for now and start using a diary for further compliments once you run out of space here.

NOTES:

_____

_____

_____

_____

_____

_____

_____

_____

_____

_____

_____

_____

Keep such diary for at least a month and notice the changes.

If you paid attention, I did not specify what compliment or what kind of positive remark. It simply does not matter. Any remark or compliment whether regarding your appearance, character or abilities will do, as it is about the effect such action has on you, i.e. any remark makes you feel great about yourself.

The Benefit of Exercise 1.

Open the diary anytime you feel down or you want to remind yourself why you are so great, and re-read all you wrote down.

Keep recording any special remarks you ever get towards yourself, that way your diary will be an unlimited resource: like a recording of *positive feelings* you can replay to make you feel great about yourself.

Now choose one person who unconditionally loves you and thinks great of you.

Take your time, but choose only one.

Great! We shall ask this person to help you. How? You know how sometimes you think of an old friend and shortly the phone rings? Or you thought of a friend you wanted to meet for some time, only to arrive to the party and to find that very friend there. We shall use a similar 'sense' technique here.

We are not asking them directly, we sense (imagine) they are next to us.

Excellent, you are ready for the next exercise.

Just before you start, make sure you have a glass of water handy. It is a very strong and powerful exercise and should you get overwhelmed, you will have to stop the exercise, have some water, relax and then continue.

Many of my coachees get an unexpected rush of emotions by doing this exercise yet it is the most amazing exercise you can perform to give an instant boost to your *self-esteem* and *confidence*.

I used it many times myself to keep my mind clear and concentrate on my future actions. In fact it was the main exercise and the only one I did for a first month after my former husband passed away to keep myself on track.

I still use it occasionally when I need to take a serious decision and I am not entirely sure what direction to take.

You can do it with open or closed eyes as it really does not matter; whichever works for you best.

Exercise 2.

It would be ideal if you are alone in the room and if you can close your eyes. Better yet, pick in the room a position where you are and where the chosen person is.

Physically, position yourself first where you would like to be (note the area), then position yourself where your chosen person is going to be (note the area).

Now move yourself to the initial position you chose for yourself, facing towards the position you chose for the other person. Take a few deep breaths in and out (2-4 times is great).

Relax.

Pay attention for a moment to what you are wearing right now, to any jewellery you might be wearing, your hair colour, feel your posture. Relax.

Imagine now (in your mind's eye) that the very person who loves you unconditionally is opposite you. The person who unconditionally loves you is close to you and looks at you with love and admiration. Please have a look at the person carefully, what colour are their clothes, what exactly is on the person, is there a smell of perfume, what shoes if any ...

Now that you are in front of the person, clearly imagine that the person you chose is saying to you all those great things about you and that you know that they really mean it.

Listen to them saying how much they respect you and how much they love you. Pay attention to how they say it to you, is the voice loud or quiet?

Remember every compliment and positive remark you hear.

Now truly enjoy all the words you have just heard. Enjoy that warmth and happiness that you are filled with. Enjoy that nice feeling of knowing you are loved and recognised.

Truly enjoy.

Now open your eyes or simply acknowledge your posture and where you are.

Next step is to position yourself on the chosen person's location. If you are alone in the room, please, move into the person's place and look towards your former position. Be there for a while and start imaginining you are the person who loves you unconditionally. Look at yourself with the eyes of the person who thinks highly of you. Feel you are the person. Feel those clothes, those shoes or a perfume, remember the voice and words.

Now with your mind's eye 'look' at yourself being close to you and tell yourself all those great things again.

You can say out loud or you can speak in your mind.

You are the chosen person for the time being, now saying to yourself all the great things. Saying how much you are loved and how important your very existence is.

Enjoy saying it. Give yourself some time to enjoy it.

Now open your eyes or simply pay attention to your posture if you had your eyes open during the exercise.

Go back to your initial position.

Feel your own clothes now, feel your own shoes or accessories, feel the temperature in the room. Relax and imagine the person you chose is still in front of you and still saying all those great things — how much you are loved and how great you are.

Listen. Enjoy.

... and take a few deep breaths in and out (2-4 times) and come back to your normal senses.

Notice things around you.

Have a sip of water.

The Benefit of Exercise 2.

How nice it is to know you are always loved and you always matter. Keep that feeling you have just re-lived with yourself at all times.

Replay that exercise in your mind whenever you are looking for support.

Replay the exercise whenever you want to know you are loved.

You are loved.

Write down those great compliments and statements regarding how special you are and how loved you are into your diary as well.

NOTES:

_____

_____

_____

_____

_____

_____

_____

_____

_____

_____

_____

_____

_____

_____

You have just received a major *confidence* boost 'injection'. Whenever you need another 'injection' like this, open the diary and read it before approaching the action you are about to take.

We can go even further ...

Take the diary which already has the compliments you have received from others and the very special person who loves you unconditionally and:

Exercise 3.

Write in your diary five sentences why you respect yourself.

A little help here ☺ It doesn't matter what you respect yourself for: it can be your perfect manicure or the fact you are always on time for business meetings.

Maybe it's just the way you perfectly tie your shoe laces... or that you are a great parent.

NOTES:

_____

_____

_____

_____

_____

_____

_____

_____

_____

_____

_____

_____

_____

_____

Let's admit there must be something you respect yourself for.

Write in the present tense a short positive statement, for example:

> I respect myself because I prepare thoroughly before meeting my clients.
> I respect myself for overcoming obstacles.
> I respect myself for looking after my parents.
> I respect myself for helping others.
> I respect myself for being a great parent.
> I respect myself for taking the best actions I can, given the circumstances.

Write the statement corresponding the most to you.

Now write five sentences why you love yourself.

For example, you might love yourself because you have beautiful eyes or a charming smile.

You might love yourself for being a reliable friend.

You might love yourself for ...

Write what comes to your mind first and makes you feel great about yourself.

NOTES:

_____

_____

_____

_____

_____

_____

_____

_____

_____

_____

_____

The Benefit of Exercise 3.

It is as important to love yourself as to understand and recognise others love you too.

As I constantly mention to all my coachees:

> 'How do people know they can love you and respect you if YOU do not love or respect yourself?'

Let's go back just a bit. Are you aware of what *confidence* stands for?

We know why you need *confidence*, but what is that?

Most people when asked get really confused... and rather than giving an answer, instead talk about why it is important.

Let me help you:

> *Confidence* is a state and a positive state, as it is about being positive in regard to what you can do and not worrying over what you can't do.

Such an explanation will help you agree with the statement that a confident person is open to learning, because one knows that one's confidence allows the person to open one of life's doors after another, eager to discover what waits on the other side.

The confident person knows that every new unknown is an opportunity to learn more about yourself and to release your ability. Confident people do not concentrate on their weaknesses; they develop and maximise their strengths.

There is an amazing saying I've been told by a colleague. That the words "should" and "shouldn't" are "dirty" words because they imply that we are behaving in accordance with someone else wishes and not our own real desires.

How often did you make steps in life because you felt you should? How often did you take time to see what you are really great at? Are you great at management? Are you great at playing piano? Are you great at keeping the house in order? Are you doing what you are great at or are you doing something you wrongly chose and constantly strangling to improve yourself at it?

It is an amazing confidence booster when you are great at what you do.

What is it you are great at? What are you mediocre at?

Remember the world does not need mediocre — as we can all admit, everyone can be mediocre at many things.

For example you have some skills which you can rate on a scale of 1 to 10. Some skills, let's say playing the piano would be 5 and you would get 8 at being an entrepreneur. Now imagine you have decided to develop your piano skills further.

You would get a tutor, you would invest a lot of time into it and as a result of your efforts, time and money would be diverted to increasing your skills in playing piano to about 6, or maybe 7?

Now on the other hand imagine if you would invest all that into becoming a better, smarter, wealthier entrepreneur? There is a great chance you would reach a mark of 9 on the scale... maybe even 10?

It is all about where your attention goes. It is also about recognising your unique qualities and giving it most of your attention.

This world wants 10s.

As you know the problem is that everyone is so used to developing our weak sides that we neglect our strengths. By developing our weaker sides not only are we constantly stuck in a negative state, as we are in a constant fight with ourselves and the expectations built by others, but we deny ourselves true appreciation. We feel unloved. We feel unrecognised. We feel we are not being our best.

Take your time NOW, recognise your strengths.

Start enjoying your life.

Start accomplishing a lot!

Note down at least five of your strengths right now, before continuing further:

NOTES:

_____

_____

_____

_____

_____

_____

_____

_____

_____

_____

_____

_____

Confident people also make a habit of thinking and acting positively.

Now that you know you have unique qualities or you are on the path of discovering them you might have a strong confidence boost for a short time only to be stumbled with the question:

> Well, if I am so great, why am I not achieving the results I am after?

And as you might know already that is where the confidence comes in.

Have you ever paid attention how huge an airplane is while waiting for boarding or maybe watching airplanes on TV? I mean the airplane which is stationary and does not move.

Now remember boarding the plane or watching others do it. Everyone is comfortable, placing their bags into overhead compartments and positioning themselves comfortably and waiting for this large airplane to take off.

What do you think the airplane needs in order to take off? In order to start it's engines working, even to start moving?

Exactly! The fuel.

Without fuel, that very large airplane sitting on a runway, which can fly long distances and is very strong, can not move even a bit.

It needs fuel to fly.

As do we.

We need our *confidence*, like the airplane fuel, to release all the huge talents we have inside ourselves. We need *confidence* to show the the world how amazing we are and we need *confidence* to release our full potential.

So what is *confidence*?

Confidence is generally described as a state of being certain either that a hypothesis or prediction is correct or that a chosen course of action is the best or most effective.

Now think about the statement for a while. Prediction? You are losing sleep or are anxious regarding something that hasn't even happened yet?

There is of course an explanation for such a phenomenon and it is related to our schemas, mental structures we build that represent some aspects of the world. Schemas are structures that organise our knowledge and assumptions about something and are used for easier and speedier interpretation and processing of the information.

We cannot deny the benefits presented by schemas. Can you imagine trying to figure out how to open a door every time that you are in front of one? Yet we have to recognise that some schemas can block our progress, or even worse diminish our self-worth.

Did you pay attention to the word: "assumptions"?

Yes, we do not feel confident regarding this or that situation, or quality, or character trait because we are trying to predict and assume.

Our confidence is our belief that we can succeed. Our confidence gets us started and helps us finish many challenges we are faced with in life.

Without *confidence* we live in fear and feel unfulfilled.

Pick up the notebook you wrote your statements in regarding yourself earlier on. Read them again and recognise you feel more confident now.

You already did a lot. You are learning even more. You constantly develop your *confidence*.

Confident people differ from non-confident as they know they are loved. And that is the amazing part of the confidence. When you know you are loved you feel safe, you feel needed and you feel supported. You feel recognised in some sense or another when you know you are loved.

Everyone desires and needs love and acceptance from others.

It is our human nature.

Of course there is no way every single person will love and accept you, yet there are many people who love you already!

Turn your attention to those who accept you already. Turn your attention to those who love you already. They will reinforce that special feeling of acceptance and you will radiate that. Just by this simple action you will attract more amazing people into your life.

On the other hand, how do you know that the people you think do not love you or do not respect you, do not in fact love you and respect you?

There is a classic case I have experienced in my early coaching days when working with a few heterosexual couples which should give you a small insight and help you change the opinion regarding the people that you think do not love or accept you.

It is very common for a male partner to state that he likes to hear that he is loved, or as we say, "he loves with his ears". Therefore he constantly gives his partner compliments.

For a female partner it is common for her to say that she loves being showed that she is loved, and therefore she always gets presents for her male partner.

Pay attention - such couples normally come to me for help in order to see whether they can still love each other and continue happy relationships. Each insisted they are not loved!

They have contacted me because they each insisted they loved the other.

Can you see how a simple communication issue can affect an amazing relationship?

Ok, it's not quite that simple as given the rate of divorce recently we hardly have a 'sample couple' to copy, nor does everyone have such a couple to learn from when they are a child.

Check your relationships and your friendships and especially people you think do not love you or accept you. Pay attention to what the signs are that they accept or love others? Are they the same by any chance towards you, even though they are not giving the signals that you yourself would usually project at people when you love and respect them?

If not, move on, we have so many people on the planet, surely there are more than you can handle that can or want to love you and be friends with you ☺

If you still completely don't see any solution, come and join my *workshops*, you'll be surprised at the discovery or... you'll leave with new amazing friends. Details are at www.SkinnyRichCoach.com

Or give this book as a present to a person you like though you are not yet sure about their feelings towards you. This book is a guaranteed ice breaker... well that was a joke, but you never know...

Let me give you another example, from my own life

I spent years arguing with my parents when, after observing my father for years showering my mum with presents, and saying that this is how he shows his affection, I have adopted the same pattern towards them. My father even told me one day that he recognises he is not the most affectionate man on the planet and this is the only way he knows how to show his love and appreciation to my mum (it is no longer the case though).

So I got used to the idea that I should give presents to people I love or admire.

To my huge surprise quite a few years ago, both my parents lashed out at me saying that they felt very unloved by me. They think I do not care about them and they feel isolated from me...

After all those years constantly showering them with presents?

I had no choice but to confront them and explain that is how I perceived I had to show my love towards them. And that was the day my relationship with parents moved to a new stage.

They where so shocked, they told me: "Daughter, but the way we want you to show your love to us is by spending more time with us and letting us more into your life." (I am a very private person).

Can you notice the confusion?

As children we learn to copy other people's behaviour and we adjust ourselves accordingly in order to achieve the result we seek or simply satisfy our needs. I do not just mean parents, it could be any figure we choose in order to copy their behaviour.

Again, remember schemas?

What we forget later on in life, is that we constantly need to adjust our behaviour according to the new people or new circumstances we face. Do not take for granted your old habits. Of course they have served you well!

The question here is - do they still serve you as well now? Keep the ones that do and change the ones that don't.

A little extra on the subject of relationships. I have coached several people who felt so bad regarding themselves that they were involved in relationship with people who hurt them, simply because they believed that is all they deserved. In reality you will attract a relationship that is a perfect match at every stage of your life.

If you feel yourself low and unloved you really may attract partners who will take advantage of you and support your own opinion about yourself.

If you are still looking for relationships and feel low regarding yourself, increase your *confidence* first.

Learn to love yourself first. Learn your unique qualities and then only once you feel happy with yourself, open up. You will attract the same *confident*, loving and supporting partner. It worked for every single I have coached so far and it will work for you!

And the paradox is that many people fail in relationships or in marriages because they simply don't love themselves, and therefore they have nothing to give in a relationship. They create an imbalance in the relationship and great families break down. If only they would know the solution is really easy.

You see now how beneficial is to be confident at any stage of your life or in any circumstances?

Not only you can achieve more, you can have better relationships, and not just with your family.

It is not only about getting the promotion you are after, and it is not only about taking yourself down to the gym and stretching those muscles of yours. It is not just about feeling important. *Confidence* is a great asset.

We need *confidence* just like that airplane I mentioned earlier. Otherwise we just exist, sit there and wait...

Waiting for WHAT?

I coach privately very successful people who would like to be even wealthier and more successful. You might say why? Because being confident is about taking actions and constantly keeping the right confident state. You constantly need to take new actions to feed your newly required confidence level. And yes, I have met many successful people who lack confidence in one or other aspect of their life and many of them have far from perfect relationships or even have very weak health.

I always promote the balance hence the name **Skinny Rich Coach**. It is about being wealthy yet about healthy in your life, in your relationships.

If you want to improve your relationships, your wealth and your health, start acting and start 'feeding' your *confidence*.

And keep this book as a constant reminder, you already have anything you need to succeed.

Let's just add some 'energy'.

Now we move on to "Affirmations".

Most of you know what they are, for those who never came across them or for those of you who are confused:

Affirmations are your goals.

Affirmations are statements of what we are or what we want to achieve or become.

A bit of scientific results here will help you understand the importance of affirmations:

> We know that *self-confidence* is the key to Social Intelligence and success. We also know that by believing in yourself and our own abilities we find it easier to relax and 'be yourself' in any social

situation. Which in turn (sending the right signals on subconscious level) allows others to be more relaxed next to us and enjoy our company.

John Bargh, a Social Psychologist at New York State University, decided to make an experiment in order to see whether negative age stereotypes would in any way have an effect on college students.

The experiment was the following:

One group of students had to unscramble sentences scattered with neutral words relating to age.

The second group had an identical task, except that their sentences were scattered with age-related words that were particularly negative.

Some amazing results were produced!

The students who had dealt with the negative words remembered significantly less about the experiment that the students who had sorted neutral words.

Yet, more significantly, the students who had dealt with the negative words became 'suddenly older'.

Unknown to them, their behaviour was being monitored. And as they were leaving the room after the experiment (where negative age related words were used), they were moving significantly slower as they were walking away. Even in the prime of youth, their physical appearance and movements became much closer to the negative word descriptions of old age than were those of the neutral group participants.

From this experiment, John Bargh concluded that the images stored in our minds have extraordinary power over our behaviours.

But those images do not have to be negative. They can be positive ones too.

And positive images can be just as powerful, if not more so, than negative images.

Here where the affirmations can play their vital role.

You are welcome to use the affirmation we have created together with attendees of my *confidence* workshops previously and I shall mention them in a short while.

As I stated earlier this is the only book of it's kind and rather than just providing you with affirmations I shall explain how to create your **OWN**:

NOTES:

_____

_____

_____

_____

_____

_____

_____

_____

_____

Exercise 4.

State something major you want to achieve.

At this stage it is irrelevant whether it is something you want to achieve or something you want to exclude from your life.

Now write it down.

For example if you would like to stop being unconfident, you would write something along the following lines-

'I want to stop being unconfident'.

If you are not happy you lack confidence at your work and your opinion does not get considered you would probably write something similar to-

'I want to stop being upset that my opinion does not count.'

I deliberately gave you negative examples as many times we are wishing to avoid something in our lives.

By all means you can write straight away something positive like:

'I want to be confident'.

With the goals or desires where there is a 'negative' present you need to change it to what it is exactly you want to achieve, excluding or substituting negative with positive.

For example:

> If you've mentioned 'I want to stop being unconfident',
> you change it for 'I want to become confident' or
> 'I want to be happy and ensure my opinion counts'.

Once you have decided on what you want and adjust it to the positive statement we need to make a positive statement out of it in present tense.

For example:

> I am confident!
> I am happy and my opinion always counts!

Those are the ready affirmations.
How you use affirmations:

> Write down as many goals in the affirmation form as you want, preferably ten for the first week and say them out loud. Do they sound acceptable to you?

What I mean here is that if you are really lacking in *confidence*, by stating: 'I am confident' your face muscles might get uncomfortably tense and you might feel demoralised and feel like saying 'Yeah, I wish'.

When you say affirmations out loud they should make you feel happy, positive and re-energised.

If it's not happening, adjust them ever so slightly.

For example: 'I am becoming more confident!'

Now not only would that be honest as you are reading this book and learning how to be more confident, that should make you feel you are honest with yourself.

Later when you get comfortable with such a statement, you can change it for the more radical version 'I am confident' even if you are still not quite there.

Remember this is the benefit of affirmations — they are our goals!

NOTES:

_____

_____

_____

_____

_____

_____

_____

_____

_____

_____

_____

_____

_____

_____

The Benefit of Exercise 4.

Once you have created such a list of approximately ten affirmations, keep saying it out loud if possible or in your mind at least three times every morning, lunch and in the evening before you go to sleep for the first week.

Notice the changes.

If you don't, other people will and they will comment to you about that... or even better, people will find you more *confident* and more attractive and will approach you more easily.

After a week review your affirmations and change some which are no longer relevant if necessary.

During the following weeks say them as many times as you can and just a few minutes before any situations that you feel even a tiny bit anxious about.

That will boost your *confidence* and energy level at once.

Here are the affirmations you can use meanwhile before you add or create your own created together with attendees during the previous *confidence* workshops:

> I am loved
> I know I am loved
> I am loved and respected
> I am confident
> I am happy
> I am wealthy
> I love my body
> I am outgoing
> I am recognised
> I love myself
> I respect myself
> I have great friends
> I enjoy my daily exercises

Here are some affirmations we have created with attendees during confidence workshops for business people only:

I love meeting new people
I am respected by others
I make the difference
I am successful in my relationships
I am successful in my business
I am successful in my life
I love making new friends
I built fantastic new businesses
I am reliable

I once heard this amazing story I always try to share with all my coachees:

> Many many years ago in a village somewhere in the middle of nowhere, children were told by their parents never to go to the mountain near by. Children were told that a huge, angry and very stinky monster lives there.

After many years of living in fear some brave men decided to go and see the monster for themselves and see whether they could defeat it.

So one day the whole village gathered together and the brave men were given some food, some amour and blessings.

They started their journey to the mountain.

As the men approached the bottom of the mountain, the ground started shaking and they could hear the growling sound of a huge monster. It's needless to add how horrible it smelled. Most of the men ran away screaming.

The rest who stayed, decided to continue.

Half way up the mountain they saw the monster for the first time. It was smaller than they expected, yet it was extremely loud and continued to emit such a stench it was unbearable for anyone to continue.

All except one man.

The remaining man said to himself: 'I am going to defeat the monster' and continued on his way.

The closer he got to the monster, the smaller the monster seemed to become.

At one stage the monster seemed to be the size of the man. The man continued and as he came closer, the monster shrank so much in size that the man could pick it up and place it in the middle of his palm.

Once he had a closer look at the monster the man asked him 'Well, then, who are you?'

In a very very tiny voice the monster whispered: "I am your Fear".

It is the same in our lives, so many things or actions seem so scary or monstrous or horrible until we begin to confront it. And the more we confront it the smaller it becomes.

It seems that fear is a part of our everyday life today.

Please answer: What is it you are afraid of?

Why exactly do you experience fear right now (towards something or someone)? Why not to change the feeling of fear for a feeling of excitement?

Feelings are ever-changing!

Let's just stop here for a moment. Did you realise 'fear' is a feeling? You simply feel it inside.

That means you are afraid of a feeling?

Think about it:

should you be intimidated by a mere feeling?

Some may attach fears to previous failures.

Become more *confident*. Do not see setbacks as failures. A person is not a failure because tries some things and it does not work out. Would you consider Richard Branson a failure? Remember his attempts to fly hot air-balloon?

You only fail when you stop trying. Sometimes you may need to try even more than King Robert the Bruce did ☺

Instead of allowing mistakes to stop you — let them train you.

I always mention to my coachees that if I try something and it does not work, at least I know not to try it again under the same circumstances or adjust my actions accordingly.

And why on earth would you not like yourself so much? Why do you constantly compare yourself with other people?

No matter how good we look or how talented we are. No matter how smart or how successful we are, there will be always someone better and sooner or later we will run into them. Just accept it.

Confidence is found in doing the best we can with what we have to work with and not comparing ourselves with others. It is not about competing with others, it is about you succeeding in what you want to achieve.

Our true joys lie not in being better than others but in being the best we can be.

Advertising is often geared to make people strive to look the best

- ❖ the best car!
- ❖ buy it and you will be number one!
- ❖ the best clothes!
- ❖ buy them and people will really admire you!

It is about you! People will be attracted to you because of your character and your *confidence*, because of the way you are.

Car, clothes and other material goods are great — for our own pleasure! I am a well known shopaholic. I love great clothes or unique designs, yet my confidence level is independent of them and my friends will gladly confirm it to you. In fact they love the very fact I can be glammed up for a dinner party and the next morning be covered in dirt flying kites on Hampstead Heath... wearing torn clothes.

Only when you build your *confidence* from the inside out, then you will appear to be confident. The clothes, cars, restaurants... all extras ... and for your own pleasure.

We are physical beings too, therefore it is advisable to admire and enjoy everything the material world has to offer. Yet the purpose of this book is to help you build your confidence from inside.

And if you are one of those people who wants to have a good life, great cars, a beautiful partner — believe me — I understand and support your desires!

If you are one of the people who believe that material things are our enemies, I urge you to realise the material beauty you are surrounded with and change your view. And by that I mean, notice anything material or physical that you are surrounded with:

> flowers, trees, a nicely designed road sign, the linen for your kitchen table, cars on roads, the chair you sit in, the beautiful house you saw yesterday...

Once you are confident, you have the real opportunity to have anything you want to have, to achieve anything you want to achieve, to have the great relationships you want to have and to have the income you want to have.

Just be the person you WANT to BE.

Exercise 5.

This is a very powerful and useful exercise and very popular in neuro-lingustic programming.

You can do it anywhere yet for best results, it is preferable to be alone with no distracting sounds. You can even put a soft melody to play on the background.

Position yourself comfortably yet alert. Take 2-3 deep breaths in and out.

Relax.

Think of the moment you were really confident last time.

Think well, try to remember all the details of the event or situation when you felt really confident last time.

Now close your eyes and in your mind's eye imagine you are reliving that very moment.

You are in that moment. You feel incredibly confident.

Look around. Notice what you are wearing. Notice if you are alone or there are other people. If there are other people what are they saying to you? What was the temperature like at that moment? Was it room temperature or were you outside?

Now that you are reliving that moment and feeling incredibly confident, just like using a TV remote control, increase your confidence level, increase the brightness level, increase the sounds you hear ever so slightly.

Enjoy feeling that increased confidence and feel empowered.

Truly enjoy the *confident* state.

Now reduce the feeling of confidence on your remote control, reduce the brightness and switch off any sounds.

Take 2-3 deep breaths in and out.

Open your eyes.

Have a drink if possible.

Now think of the moment when you felt even more confident.

When you thought of yourself: Wow! I am really great, I feel so confident.

You can even use someone else as a dummy in a sense, if you would ever want to feel like a particular person during some moment when they were feeling exceptionally confident — let's say winning a particular award. In which case you can relive their confidence moment. Choose the one you would like to re-experience... let's start.

Close your eyes. Think of that moment when you were even more confident than the previous one. And re-live it.

If you chose someone else, use your imagination and re-live their moment of confidence as if you yourself were experiencing it.

In your mind's eyes imagine you are re-living that very moment when you felt so confident.

Notice what you wear, notice people around you, or maybe you were alone. Notice if there are any smells, if the water is near by or if you are in a room. Feel that confidence increasing inside yourself.

Now take that imaginary remote control and increase that very feeling of confidence just a little bit.

Now increase it more, now make it really loud. Increase the smells' intensity if there were any, increase the air temperature, increase the brightness of your confidence.

Enjoy 'bathing' in that extreme feeling of confidence.

Now 'turn' down a bit the confidence, reduce even more, make the colours around you fuzzier and slowly open your eyes.

Look around.

Repeat this exercise as often as you need to.

The Benefit of Exercise 5.

By performing this exercise you put your mind in a *confident* state independent of the surrounding situation. It is especially great to re-play a few times before attending an important meeting.

If you pay attention, you will notice that even your posture changes when you re-play that moment. You will start sending out signals of great confidence on subconscious level that in return will make other people believe in you easier and faster.

I have heard a saying there are two types of people in the world:

> the ones who wait for something to happen and
> the ones who make something happen.

I tend to agree after working with so many people and would love to add some people are naturally shy, while others are naturally bold.

Yet we all have something to overcome.

A naturally bold person has to overcome pride, excessive aggression and false confidence, while the naturally shy must overcome anxiety, the temptation to withdraw from challenges and low confidence.

No matter what type you are closer too, you have to take actions to stay confident.

Yes, the world is **filled** with people who feel empty and unfulfilled because they have spent their lives complaining about what they did not have, instead of using what they do have already.

Do not spend your life in the tyranny of 'if only'. If only I had more money. If only I was born there. If only my parents would give me better education. If only I was taller...

Remember, where the mind goes, the person follows. If you pay attention to your thoughts and choose to think of things that will help you instead of hinder you...

Think yourself *confident* and you will be *confident*.

Postscript

I'd like to ask **you** to promote this book.

Go to www.SkinnyRichCoach.com where you will find the link for the book you can send to your friends and colleagues or visit any major book retailers.

Lack of confidence is a common problem for many people and not only prevents you from progressing in your life and career but also makes you feel lonely and diminishes your self-worth.

Help others to overcome these fears and gain confidence before anxieties or fears take over and tell them about this book.

If you would like to experience the group work on confidence where you built your own mini action plan at the end, please visit our page with Seminars and Workshops at www.SkinnyRichCoach.com or contact for further details.

For FREE EXTRA RESOURCES as well as invitations to events, sign up to our newsletter by filling in the Contact form via www.2skinny2rich.com

**EVERYONE deserves to be recognised in this world.
The most important person in the world is YOU.**

For other books and CDs, follow us on:

http://www.facebook.com/pages/Skinny-Rich-Coach/
332427907358
http://twitter.com/SkinnyRichCoach
www.SkinnyRichCoach.com